Impressum
Verlag: BABADADA GmbH, Nedderfeld 112 , 22529 Hamburg
Geschäftsführer / Verlagsleitung: Harald Hof
Druck: Books on Demand GmbH, In de Tarpen 42, 22848 Norderstedt

Imprint
Publisher: BABADADA GmbH, Nedderfeld 112 , 22529 Hamburg, Germany
Managing Director / Publishing direction: Harald Hof
Print: Books on Demand GmbH, In de Tarpen 42, 22848 Norderstedt

classroom
aula

divide
dividir

186/2

board
pizarrón

school yard
patio de escuela

teacher
maestro

paper
papel

write
escribir

pen
birome

desk
escritorio

ruler
regla

book
libro

pupil
alumno

satchel

mochila

pencil case

caja de lápices

pencil

lápiz

pencil sharpener

sacapuntas

rubber

goma (de borrar)

drawing pad

bloc de dibujo

drawing

dibujo

paintbrush

pincel

paint box

caja de pinturas

scissors

tijera

glue

pegamento

exercise book

cuaderno de ejercicios

homework

tarea

number

número

add

sumar

subtract

restar

multiply

multiplicar

calculate

calcular

letter

letra

alphabet

abecedario

word

palabra

text

texto

read

leer

chalk

tiza

lesson

lección

register

cuaderno de clase

exam

examen

certificate

certificado

school uniform

uniforme escolar

education

educación

encyclopedia

enciclopedia

university

universidad

microscope

microscopio

map

mapa

paper bin

tacho (de basura)

hotel
hotel

Grand

hostel
hostel

ROOMS

bureau de change
casa de cambio

ECHANGE

suitcase
valija

car
auto

language

idioma

yoɛ / no

sí / no

Okay

Está bien

hello

hola

translator

traductor

Thank you

Gracias

how much does … cost?

¿cuánto cuesta…?

I do not understand

No entiendo

problem

problema

Good evening!

¡Buenas tardes!

Good morning!

¡Buenos días!

Good night!

¡Buenas noches!

bye bye

adiós

direction

dirección

luggage

equipaje

bag

bolso

backpack

mochila

guest

invitado

room

habitación

sleeping bag

bolsa de dormir

tent

carpa

tourist information

información turística

beach

playa

credit card

tarjeta de crédito

breakfast

desayuno

lunch

almuerzo

dinner

cena

ticket

pasaje

lift

ascensor

stamp

sello

border

frontera

customs

aduana

embassy

embajada

visa

visa

passport

pasaporte

aeroplane
avión

ship
barco

fire engine
autobomba

truck
camión

bus
colectivo

motorboat
lancha a motor

car
auto

bike
bicicleta

ferry

ferry

boat

bote

motorbike

moto

police car

patrullero

racing car

auto de carreras

rental car

auto de alquiler

car sharing

alquiler de autos

breakdown truck

grúa

refuse truck

camión de basura

motor

motor

fuel

nafta

petrol station

estación de servicio

traffic sign

señal de tránsito

traffic

tránsito

traffic jam

embotellamiento

car park

estacionamiento

train station

estación de tren

tracks

vías

train

tren

tram

tranvía

carriage

vagón

helicopter

helicóptero

airport

aeropuerto

tower

torre

passenger

pasajero

container

contenedor

carton

caja de cartón

cart

carretilla

basket

canasta

take off / land

despegar / aterrizar

city

ciudad

village

pueblo

city centre

centro de ciudad

house

casa

cinema
cine

advert
publicidad

street light
farol

street
calle

taxi
taxi

snack shop
kiosco

CINEMA

pedestrian
peatón

pavement
vereda

zebra crossing
paso peatonal

bin
contenedor de basura

crossing
cruce

traffic lights
semáforo

hut
cabaña

flat
departamento

train station
estación de tren

town hall
municipalidad

museum
museo

school
colegio

university

universidad

bank

banco

hospital

hospital

hotel

hotel

pharmacy

farmacia

office

oficina

book shop

librería

shop

negocio

florist's

florería

supermarket

supermercado

market

mercado

department store

grandes tiendas

fishmonger's

pescadería

shopping centre

centro comercial

harbour

puerto

park

parque

bench

banco

bridge

puente

stairs

escaleras

underground

subte

tunnel

túnel

bus stop

parada del colectivo

bar

bar

restaurant

restaurante

postbox

buzón

road sign

letrero

parking meter

parquímetro

zoo

zoológico

swimming pool

pileta

mosque

mezquita

farm

granja

pollution

contaminación

graveyard

cementerio

church

iglesia

playground

juegos infantiles

temple

templo

landscape

paisaje

leaf
hoja

signpost
poste indicador

way
camino

meadow
pradera

stone
piedra

hiker
excursionista

tree
árbol

river
río

grass
hierba

flower
flor

valley
valle

hill
montaña

lake
lago

forest
bosque

desert
desierto

volcano
volcán

castle
castillo

rainbow
arco iris

mushroom
champiñón

palm tree
palmera

mosquito
mosquito

fly
mosca

ant
hormiga

bee
abeja

spider
araña

beetle

escarabajo

frog

rana

squirrel

ardilla

hedgehog

erizo

hare

liebre

owl

lechuza

bird

pájaro

swan

cisne

boar

jabalí

deer

ciervo

moose

alce

dam

presa

wind turbine

aerogenerador

solar panel

panel solar

climate

clima

waiter
mozo

menu
menú

chair
silla

soup
sopa

pizza
pizza

tablecloth
mantel

cutlery
cubiertos

starter
entrada

main course
plato principal

dessert
postre

drinks
bebidas

food
comida

bottle
botella

fast food

comida rápida

street food

comida callejera

teapot

tetera

sugar bowl

azucarera

portion

porción

espresso machine

cafetera expreso

high chair

sillita alta

bill

cuenta

tray

bandeja

knife

cuchillo

fork

tenedor

spoon

cuchara

teaspoon

cucharita

serviette

servilleta

glass

vaso

plate

plato

soup plate

plato hondo

saucer

plato

sauce

salsa

salt cellar

salero

pepper mill

molinillo de pimienta

vinegar

vinagre

oil

aceite

spices

especias

ketchup

kétchup

mustard

mostaza

mayonnaise

mayonesa

supermarket
supermercado

special offer
oferta especial

customer
cliente

dairy
lácteos

FOR

fruit
fruta

trolley
changuito

butcher's
carnicería

baker's
panadería

weigh
pesar

vegetables
verduras

meat
carne

frozen food
alimentos congelados

cold meat

fiambres

tinned food

alimentos enlatados

washing powder

detergente en polvo

sweets

golosinas

household products

electrodomésticos

cleaning products

productos de limpieza

salesperson

vendedora

till

caja

cashier

cajero

shopping list

lista de compras

opening hours

horario de atención

wallet

billetera

credit card

tarjeta de crédito

bag

cartera

plastic bag

bolsa de plástico

water

agua

juice

jugo

milk

leche

coke

bebida cola

wine

vino

beer

cerveza

alcohol

alcohol

cocoa

cacao

tea

té

coffee

café

espresso

café expreso

cappuccino

cappuccino

banana

banana

apple

manzana

orange

naranja

melon

melón

lemon

limón

carrot

zanahoria

garlic

ajo

bamboo

bambú

onion

cebolla

mushroom

champiñón

nuts

nueces

noodles

fideos

spaghetti

tallarines

rice

arroz

salad

ensalada

chips

papas fritas

fried potatoes

papas fritas

pizza

pizza

hamburger

hamburguesa

sandwich

sándwich

cutlet

churrasco

ham

jamón

salami

salame

sausage

salchicha

chicken

pollo

roast

asado

fish

pescado

porridge oats

copos de avena

muesli

muesli

cornflakes

copos de maíz

flour

harina

croissant

medialuna

bread roll

pancito

bread

pan

toast

tostada

biscuits

galletitas

butter

manteca

curd

cuajada

cake

torta

egg

huevo

fried egg

huevo frito

cheese

queso

ice cream

helado

sugar

azúcar

honey

miel

jam

mermelada

chocolate spread

pasta de chocolate

curry

curry

food - comida

farmhouse
granja

barn
granero

straw bale
fardo de paja

field
campo

horse
caballo

trailer
remolque

foal
potrillo

tractor
tractor

donkey
burro

lamb
cordero

sheep
oveja

goat

cabra

cow

vaca

calf

ternero

pig

cerdo

piglet

lechón

bull

toro

goose
ganso

duck
pato

chick
pollo

hen
gallina

cock
gallo

rat
rata

cat
gato

mouse
ratón

ox
buey

dog
perro

doghouse
cucha

garden hose
manguera

watering can
regadera

scythe
guadaña

plough
arado

sickle

hoz

hoe

azada

pitchfork

horquilla

axe

hacha

wheelbarrow

carretilla

trough

abrevadero

milk can

lechera

sack

bolsa

fence

reja

stable

establo

greenhouse

invernadero

soil

suelo

seed

semilla

fertilizer

fertilizador

combine harvester

cosechadora

farm - granja

harvest
cosechar

harvest
cosecha

yams
batatas

wheat
trigo

soy
soja

potato
papa

corn
maíz

rapeseed
semilla de colza

fruit tree
árbol frutal

cassava
mandioca

cereals
cereales

chimney
chimenea

roof
techo

drain pipe
caño de desagüe

window
ventana

garage
garaje

doorbell
timbre

door
puerta

rubbish bin
tacho de basura

letterbox
buzón

garden
jardín

living room
living

bathroom
baño

kitchen
cocina

bedroom
dormitorio

child's room
cuarto de los chicos

dining room
comedor

floor

piso

wall

pared

ceiling

cielorraso

cellar

sótano

sauna

sauna

balcony

balcón

terrace

terraza

pool

pileta

lawn mower

cortadora de pasto

sheet

sábana

bedspread

acolchado

bed

cama

broom

escoba

bucket

balde

switch

interruptor

wallpaper
empapelado

picture
imagen

lamp
lámpara

shelf
estante

cupboard
armario

television
televisión

fireplace
chimenea

flower
flor

cushion
almohadón

sofa
sofá

vase
florero

remote control
control remoto

carpet
alfombra

curtain
cortina

table
mesa

chair
silla

rocking chair
mecedora

armchair
sillón

book

libro

blanket

frazada

decoration

decoración

firewood

leña

film

película

hi-fi equipment

equipo de música

key

llave

newspaper

diario

painting

pintura

poster

póster

radio

radio

notepad

cuaderno

hoover

aspiradora

cactus

cactus

candle

vela

fridge
heladera

microwave oven
microondas

kitchen scales
balanza de cocina

toaster
tostadora

detergent
detergente

oven
horno

freezer
freezer

rubbish bin
tacho de basura

dishwasher
lavaplatos

cooker

cocina

pot

olla

cast-iron pot

olla de hierro fundido

wok / kadai

wok

pan

sartén

kettle

pava

steamer

vaporera

baking tray

bandeja de horno

crockery

vajilla

mug

taza

bowl

bol

chopsticks

palitos

ladle

cucharón

spatula

estpátula

whisk

batidora

strainer

colador

sieve

colador

grater

rallador

mortar

mortero

barbecue

parrilla

open fire

fogata

chopping board

tabla de picar

rolling pin

palo de amasar

corkscrew

sacacorchos

can

lata

can opener

abrelatas

pot holder

manopla

sink

pileta

brush

cepillo

sponge

esponja

blender

batidora

deep freezer

congelador

baby bottle

mamadera

tap

canilla

heating
calefacción

shower
ducha

towel
toalla

shower curtain
cortina de ducha

bubble bath
baño de espuma

bathtub
bañadera

glass
vaso

washing machine
lavarropas

tiles
baldosas

tap
canilla

potty
pelela

sink
pileta

toilet

inodoro

squat toilet

letrina

bidet

bidé

urinal

mingitorio

toilet paper

papel higiénico

toilet brush

cepillo para el inodoro

toothbrush

cepillo de dientes

toothpaste

dentífrico

dental floss

hilo dental

wash

lavar

handheld shower

ducha de mano

douche

ducha higiénica

basin

palangana

back brush

cepillo para espalda

soap

jabón

shower gel

gel de ducha

shampoo

shampoo

flannel

toallita

drain

desagüe

cream

crema

deodorant

desodorante

mirror

espejo

hand mirror

espejito

razor

maquinita de afeitar

shaving foam

espuma de afeitar

aftershave

aftershave

comb

peine

brush

cepillo

hair dryer

secador de pelo

hairspray

spray

makeup

maquillaje

lipstick

lápiz de labios

nail varnish

esmalte para uñas

cotton wool

algodón

nail scissors

tijera para uñas

perfume

perfume

washbag

portacosméticos

stool

banqueta

weighing scale

balanza

bathrobe

bata

rubber gloves

guantes de goma

tampon

tampón

sanitary towel

toallita femenina

chemical toilet

baño químico

alarm clock
despertador

cuddly toy
peluche

toy car
coche de juguete

rattle
sonajero

doll's house
casa de muñecas

present
regalo

balloon

globo

bed

cama

pram

cochecito

deck of cards

cartas

jigsaw

rompecabezas

comic

historieta

lego bricks

piezas de lego

building blocks

ladrillos de juguete

action figure

figura de acción

romper suit

enterito (de bebé)

Frisbee

frisbee

mobile

móvil para bebés

board game

juego de mesa

dice

dados

model train set

tren eléctrico

dummy

chupete

party

fiesta

picture book

libro de cuentos ilustrado

ball

pelota

doll

muñeca

play

jugar

sandpit

arenero

swing

hamaca

toys

juguetes

video game console

consola de videojuegos

tricycle

triciclo

teddy bear

osito de peluche

wardrobe

armario

clothing

ropa

socks

medias

stockings

medias panty

tights

calzas

scarf
bufanda

belt
cinturón

umbrella
paraguas

t-shirt
remera

boots
botas

slippers
pantuflas

trainers
zapatillas

sandals
sandalias

shoes
zapatos

rubber boots
botas de goma

underpants
ropa interior

bra
corpiño

vest
chaleco

clothing - ropa

body

body

trousers

pantalones

jeans

jeans

skirt

pollera

blouse

blusa

shirt

camisa

pullover

pulóver

hoodie

buzo

blazer

blazer

jacket

campera

coat

tapado

raincoat

piloto

costume

traje

dress

vestido

wedding dress

vestido de novia

suit

traje

nightgown

camisón

pyjamas

pijama

sari

sari

headscarf

pañuelo para cabeza

turban

turbante

burqa

burka

kaftan

caftán

abaya

abaya

swimsuit

traje de baño

trunks

short de baño

shorts

shorts

tracksuit

jogging

apron

delantal

gloves

guantes

button

botón

glasses

anteojos

bracelet

pulsera

necklace

collar

ring

anillo

earring

aro

cap

gorra

coat hanger

percha

hat

sombrero

tie

corbata

zipper

cierre

helmet

casco

braces

tiradores

school uniform

uniforme escolar

uniform

uniforme

bib

babero

dummy

chupete

nappy

pañal

server
servidor

filing cabinet
archivero

printer
impresora

monitor
monitor

paper
papel

mouse
mouse

desk
escritorio

folder
carpeta

keyboard
teclado

paper bin
tacho (de basura)

chair
silla

computer
computadora

coffee mug

taza de café

calculator

calculadora

internet

internet

laptop

laptop

letter

carta

message

mensaje

mobile

celular

network

red

photocopier

fotocopiadora

software

software

telephone

teléfono

plug socket

tomacorriente

fax machine

fax

form

formulario

document

documento

buy
comprar

pay
pagar

trade
hacer negocios

money
dinero

USD

dollar
dólar

EUR

euro
euro

JPY

yen
yen

RUB

rouble
rublo

CHF

Swiss franc
franco suizo

CNY

renminbi yuan
yuan

INR

rupee
rupia

cashpoint
cajero automático

bureau de change

casa de cambio

gold

oro

silver

plata

oil

petróleo

energy

energía

price

precio

contract

contrato

tax

impuesto

stock

acción

work

trabajar

employee

empleado

employer

empleador

factory

fábrica

shop

negocio

police officer
policía

fireman
bombero

cook
cocinero

doctor
médico

pilot
piloto

gardonor
jardinero

carpenter
carpintero

seamstress
modista

judge
juez

chemist
farmacéutico

actor
actor

bus driver

colectivero

taxi driver

taxista

fisherman

pescador

cleaning lady

mucama

roofer

techista

waiter

mozo

hunter

cazador

painter

pintor

baker

panadero

electrician

electricista

builder

albañil

engineer

ingeniero

butcher

carnicero

plumber

plomero

postman

cartero

soldier

soldado

architect

arquitecto

cashier

cajero

florist

florista

hairdresser

peluquero

conductor

cobrador

mechanic

mecánico

captain

capitán

dentist

dentista

scientist

científico

rabbi

rabino

imam

imán

monk

monje

clergyman

sacerdote

hammer
martillo

pliers
tenaza

screwdriver
destornillador

spanner
llave

torch
linterna

digger

excavadora

toolbox

caja de herramientas

ladder

escalera portátil

saw

sierra

nails

clavos

drill

taladro

repair
arreglar

shovel
pala de jardín

Damn!
¡Qué bronca!

dustpan
pala de plástico

paint pot
tacho de pintura

screws
tornillos

musical instruments
instrumentos musicales

loudspeaker
parlante

drum kit
batería

guitar
guitarra

double bass
contrabajo

trumpet
trompeta

piano
piano

violin
violín

bass
bajo

timpani
timbales

drums
tambor

keyboard
teclado

saxophone
saxofón

flute
flauta

microphone
micrófono

entrance
entrada

tiger
tigre

cage
jaula

zebra
cebra

animal feed
alimento para animales

panda
oso panda

animals

animales

elephant

elefante

kangaroo

canguro

rhino

rinoceronte

gorilla

gorila

bear

oso

camel

camello

ostrich

avestruz

lion

león

monkey

mono

flamingo

flamenco

parrot

loro

polar bear

oso polar

penguin

pingüino

shark

tiburón

peacock

pavo real

snake

serpiente

crocodile

cocodrilo

zookeeper

cuidador del zoológico

seal

foca

jaguar

jaguar

pony

poni

leopard

leopardo

hippo

hipopótamo

giraffe

jirafa

eagle

águila

boar

jabalí

fish

pescado

turtle

tortuga

walrus

morsa

fox

zorro

gazelle

gacela

American football
fútbol americano

cycling
ciclismo

tennis
tenis

basketball
básquet

swimming
natación

boxing
boxeo

ice hockey
hockey sobre hielo

football

fútbol

badminton

bádminton

athletics

atletismo

handball

handball

skiing

esquí

polo

polo

laugh
reír

jump
saltar

hug
abrazar

walk
caminar

sing
cantar

dream
soñar

pray
rezar

kiss
besar

write

escribir

draw

dibujar

show

mostrar

push

presionar

give

dar

take

tomar

have
tener

do
hacer

be
ser

stand
estar parado

run
correr

pull
tirar

throw
tirar

fall
caer

lie
estar acostado

wait
esperar

carry
llevar

sit
estar sentado

get dressed
vestirse

sleep
dormir

wake up
despertar

look at

mirar

cry

llorar

stroke

acariciar

comb

peinar

talk

hablar

understand

entender

ask

preguntar

listen

escuchar

drink

beber

eat

comer

tidy up

ordenar

love

amar

cook

cocinar

drive

manejar

fly

volar

activities - actividades

sail

navegar

calculate

calcular

read

leer

learn

aprender

work

trabajar

marry

casarse

sew

coser

brush teeth

cepillarse los dientes

kill

matar

smoke

fumar

send

enviar

grandmother
abuela

grandfather
abuelo

father
padre

mother
madre

baby
bebé

daughter
hija

son
hijo

guest

invitado

aunt

tía

uncle

tío

brother

hermano

sister

hermana

forehead
frente

eye
ojo

shoulder
hombro

finger
dedo

face
cara

chin
pera

hand
mano

breast
pecho

leg
pierna

arm
brazo

baby

bebé

man

hombre

woman

mujer

girl

nena

boy

nene

head

cabeza

back

espalda

belly

panza

belly button

ombligo

toe

dedo del pie

heel

talón

bone

hueso

hip

cadera

knee

rodilla

elbow

codo

nose

nariz

bottom

cola

skin

piel

cheek

cachete

ear

oreja

lip

labio

mouth

boca

tooth

diente

tongue

lengua

brain

cerebro

heart

corazón

muscle

músculo

lung

pulmón

liver

hígado

stomach

estómago

kidneys

riñones

sex

sexo

condom

preservativo

ovum

óvulo

semen

semen

pregnancy

embarazo

body - cuerpo

menstruation

menstruación

vagina

vagina

penis

pene

eyebrow

ceja

hair

pelo

neck

cuello

body - cuerpo

hospital
hospital

ambulance
ambulancia

wheelchair
silla de ruedas

fracture
fractura

doctor

médico

emergency room

sala de guardia

nurse

enfermera

emergency

emergencia

unconscious

inconsciente

pain

dolor

injury

lesión

bleeding

hemorragia

heart attack

infarto

stroke

ACV

allergy

alergia

cough

tos

fever

fiebre

flu

gripe

diarrhoea

diarrea

headache

dolor de cabeza

cancer

cáncer

diabetes

diabetes

surgeon

cirujano

scalpel

bisturí

operation

operación

CT

TC

x-ray

rayos x

ultrasound

ecografía

face mask

barbijo

disease

enfermedad

waiting room

sala de espera

crutch

muleta

plaster

curita

bandage

venda

injection

inyección

stethoscope

estetoscopio

stretcher

camilla

clinical thermometer

termómetro

birth

nacimiento

overweight

sobrepeso

hearing aid

audífono

disinfectant

desinfectante

infection

infección

virus

virus

HIV / AIDS

VIH / SIDA

medicine

remedio

vaccination

vacunación

tablets

comprimidos

pill

pastilla anticonceptiva

emergency call

llamada de emergencia

blood pressure monitor

tensiómetro

sick / healthy

enfermo / sano

Help!

¡Ayuda!

alarm

alarma

assault

agresión

attack

ataque

danger

peligro

emergency exit

salida de emergencia

Fire!

¡Fuego!

fire extinguisher

matafuego

accident

accidente

first-aid kit

botiquín de primeros
auxilios

SOS

SOS

police

policía

Europe

Europa

North America

América del Norte

South America

América del Sur

Africa

África

Asia

Asia

Australia

Australia

Atlantic

Atlántico

Pacific

Pacífico

Indian Ocean

Océano Índico

Antarctic Ocean

Océano Antártico

Arctic Ocean

Océano Ártico

North Pole

polo norte

South Pole

polo sur

Antarctica

Antártida

Earth

Tierra

land

tierra

sea

mar

island

isla

nation

nación

state

estado

clock face

esfera

hour hand

manecilla de las horas

minute hand

minutero

second hand

segundero

What time is it?

¿Qué hora es?

day

día

time

hora

now

ahora

digital watch

reloj digital

minute

minuto

hour

hora

Monday — lunes
Wednesday — miércoles
Friday — viernes
Tuesday — martes
Saturday — sábado
Thursday — jueves
Sunday — domingo

yesterday

ayer

today

hoy

tomorrow

mañana

morning

mañana

noon

mediodía

evening

tarde

business days

días hábiles

weekend

fin de semana

rain
lluvia

rainbow
arco iris

snow
nieve

wind
viento

spring
primavera

autumn
otoño

summer
verano

winter
invierno

weather forecast

pronóstico meteorológico

thermometer

termómetro

sunshine

luz del sol

cloud

nube

fog

niebla

humidity

humedad

lightning

rayo

thunder

trueno

storm

tormenta

hail

granizo

monsoon

monzón

flood

inundación

ice

hielo

January

enero

February

febrero

March

marzo

April

abril

May

mayo

June

junio

July

julio

August

agosto

September
....
septiembre

October
....
octubre

November
....
noviembre

December
....
diciembre

shapes
formas

circle
....
círculo

square
....
cuadrado

rectangle
....
rectángulo

triangle
....
triángulo

sphere
....
esfera

cube
....
cubo

white

blanco

yellow

amarillo

orange

naranja

pink

rosa

red

rojo

purple

violeta

blue

azul

green

verde

brown

marrón

grey

gris

black

negro

a lot / a little

mucho / poco

angry / calm

enojado / tranquilo

beautiful / ugly

lindo / feo

beginning / end

principio / fin

big / small

grande / chico

bright / dark

claro / oscuro

brother / sister

hermano / hermana

clean / dirty

limpio / sucio

complete / incomplete

completo / incompleto

day / night

día / noche

dead / alive

muerto / vivo

wide / narrow

ancho / angosto

edible / inedible

comestible / no comestible

evil / nice

malo / amable

excited / bored

entusiasmado / aburrido

fat / thin

gordo / flaco

first / last

primero / último

friend / enemy

amigo / enemigo

full / empty

lleno / vacío

hard / soft

duro / blando

heavy / light

pesado / liviano

hunger / thirst

hambre / sed

sick / healthy

enfermo / sano

illegal / legal

ilegal / legal

intelligent / stupid

inteligente / estúpido

left / right

izquierda / derecha

near / far

cerca / lejos

opposites - opuestos

new / used

nuevo / usado

nothing / something

nada / algo

old / young

viejo / joven

on / off

encendido / apagado

open / closed

abierto / cerrado

quiet / loud

silencioso / ruidoso

rich / poor

rico / pobre

right / wrong

correcto / incorrecto

rough / smooth

áspero / suave

sad / happy

triste / contento

short / long

corto / largo

slow / fast

lento / rápido

wet / dry

mojado / seco

warm / cool

caliente / frío

war / peace

guerra / paz

numbers
números

0

zero
cero

1

one
uno

2

two
dos

3

three
tres

4

four
cuatro

5

five
cinco

6

six
seis

7

seven
siete

8

eight
ocho

9

nine
nueve

10

ten
diez

11

eleven
once

12

twelve

doce

13

thirteen

trece

14

fourteen

catorce

15

fifteen

quince

16

sixteen

dieciséis

17

seventeen

diecisiete

18

eighteen

dieciocho

19

nineteen

diecinueve

20

twenty

veinte

100

hundred

cicn

1.000

thousand

mil

1.000.000

million

millón

numbers - números

English

inglés

American English

inglés americano

Mandarin Chinese

chino mandarín

Hindi

hindi

Spanish

español

French

francés

Arabic

árabe

Russian

ruso

Portuguese

portugués

Bengali

bengalí

German

alemán

Japanese

japonés

I
....
yo

you
....
vos

he / she / it
....
él / ella

we
....
nosotros

you
....
ustedes

they
....
ellos

who?
....
¿quién?

what?
....
¿qué?

how?
....
¿cómo?

where?
....
¿dónde?

when?
....
¿cuándo?

name
....
nombre

behind

detrás

in

en

in front of

adelante de

over

por encima de

on

sobre

under

debajo de

beside

al lado de

between

entre

place

lugar